11/98

FRIGHTENING FISH

SEA MONSTERS

HOMER SEWARD

The Rourke Press, Inc.
Vero Beach, Florida 32964

PHOTO CREDITS
All photos © Marty Snyderman

EDITORIAL SERVICES:
Penworthy Learning Systems

Library of Congress Cataloging-in-Publication Data

Seward, Homer. 1942-
    Frightening fish / by Homer Seward.
        p. cm. — (Sea monsters)
    Includes index
    Summary: Describes various kinds of fishes which can be frightening
because they have dangerous bites, spines, or venom.
    ISBN 1-57103-236-3
    1. Fishes—Juvenile literature. 2. Poisonous fishes—Juvenile literature.
[1. Fishes. 2. Poisonous fishes. 3. Dangerous marine animals.] I. Title.
II. Series: Seward, Homer, 1942-   Sea monsters.
QL617.2.S48 1998
597—dc21   98–20298
                                                                    CIP
                                                                    AC

Printed in the USA

TABLE OF CONTENTS

FRIGHTENING FISH

The oceans are full of fish. A few of them can be really frightening.

Everyone knows that a big, toothy shark can be scary. But many other kinds of fish can be frightening, too. Some, like the lizardfish, only look scary. Others are scary because they have dangerous bites, spines, or **venom** (VEN um). Venom is the poison made by certain animals.

The crocodile fish, or giant flathead, could "star" in a monster movie.

FISH AS SEA MONSTERS

We often call animals that are big or scary "monsters." None of them, of course, is really a monster. Monsters are make-believe.

Some of the frightening fish in the oceans, though, remind us of monsters. One of them, the biggest of all fish, is the whale shark.

Two divers swim behind a whale shark, the largest fish in the world. The whale shark has monster size, but it's almost no threat to humans.

Strange-looking toadfish is armed with spines and venom glands. Look, but don't touch.

The whale shark can be up to 40 feet (12 meters) long. It surely looks like a monster! But the whale shark is harmless. It eats only tiny floating animals.

KINDS OF FRIGHTENING FISH

Another fish whose size makes it frightening is the jewfish. It weighs up to 700 pounds (318 kilograms). The jewfish often hides in undersea caves and shipwrecks.

The toadfish is less than 12 inches (31 centimeters) long. Even so, it has monster looks—wide, toothy mouth and a beard of rubbery "whiskers," called **barbels** (BAHR belz).

The frogfish, or anglerfish, looks like a sponge. It's a *little* monster. The frogfish wiggles a wormlike growth on its head. The "worm" attracts **prey** (PRAY), the animals the frogfish eat.

The jewfish can be frightening just because of its great size and toothy jaws.

SHARKS

To many people, sharks are monsters. It is true that several kinds of large sharks have attacked and killed people. But shark attacks are quite rare. People have done far more harm to sharks than sharks have to people.

Most sharks are harmless. Of about 350 **species** (SPEE sheez), or kinds, of sharks, just 70 species ever reach six feet (two meters) in length.

Perhaps the most frightening fish of all is the great white shark, which sometimes attacks humans.

STONEFISH

The stonefish is the most venomous of fish. That means the stonefish stores a very powerful venom, or poison, in its body.

The stonefish hides easily in shallow water and lies quietly. The danger is that someone may step on it.

The brightly colored stonefish is protected by the venom in its sharp spines.

Great barracuda's wolfish jaws make it look more dangerous than it is.

Stonefish venom is in its sharp spines. A spine can cause pain, or even the death of a person.

Stonefish are found only in parts of the Indian and Pacific Oceans, not along North American shores.

BARRACUDA

The barracuda looks frightening whether it wants to or not. That's because the barracuda has a jaw full of long, sharp teeth. Even when the barracuda isn't snapping at a meal, its teeth show.

Twenty species of speedy barracudas roam the seas. The longest reach five feet (one and a half meters).

Barracudas can be curious. They may swim close to a diver, but they eat fish not divers.

A barracuda lurks beneath a dive boat in the Caribbean Sea.

SCORPIONFISH

The big, wolfish barracuda is not nearly as dangerous as its looks. The scorpionfish doesn't look dangerous, but it is.

Scorpionfish are only about 12 inches (31 centimeters) long. They hide easily, because they look just like the bits of seaweed, coral, and rock around them.

Scorpionfish have spines with venom. They can cause pain if they're stepped on or handled.

The scorpionfish of Florida and the Caribbean Sea are not as dangerous as their cousins in the Indian and Pacific Oceans.

Scorpionfish are loaded with venomous spines.

LIONFISH

Lionfish belong to the scorpionfish family. Lionfish have venomous spines, too. Lionfish, though, don't blend in with their surroundings. Lionfish are brightly colored. Their colors seem to warn, "Watch out! We're dangerous."

Beneath the beauty lies a spiny beast. The lionfish, like a sea going porcupine, is loaded with venomous spines.

Like a spiny balloon, a bridled burrfish protects itself by filling up with air. Many of the inflatable fish have poisonous flesh.

It's a fair warning. Lionfish have almost as many spines (18) as you have fingers and toes. Any one of the spines can poke an enemy with a shot of venom. It's not likely to kill anyone, but it hurts terribly.

FRIGHTENING FISH AND PEOPLE

Experienced divers don't find many fish truly frightening. Rather, they find fish interesting, even if the fish are ugly, venomous, or loaded with fangs.

But experienced divers also know that nature has given fish ways to protect themselves. A fish's defense, whether spines, teeth, or just a big body, should be treated with great respect.

It is best to stay away from certain kinds of fish. That is especially true if you don't know what kind of fish you're looking at.

This eel's open jaws and sharp teeth send a clear message to divers and snorkelers: Stay back!

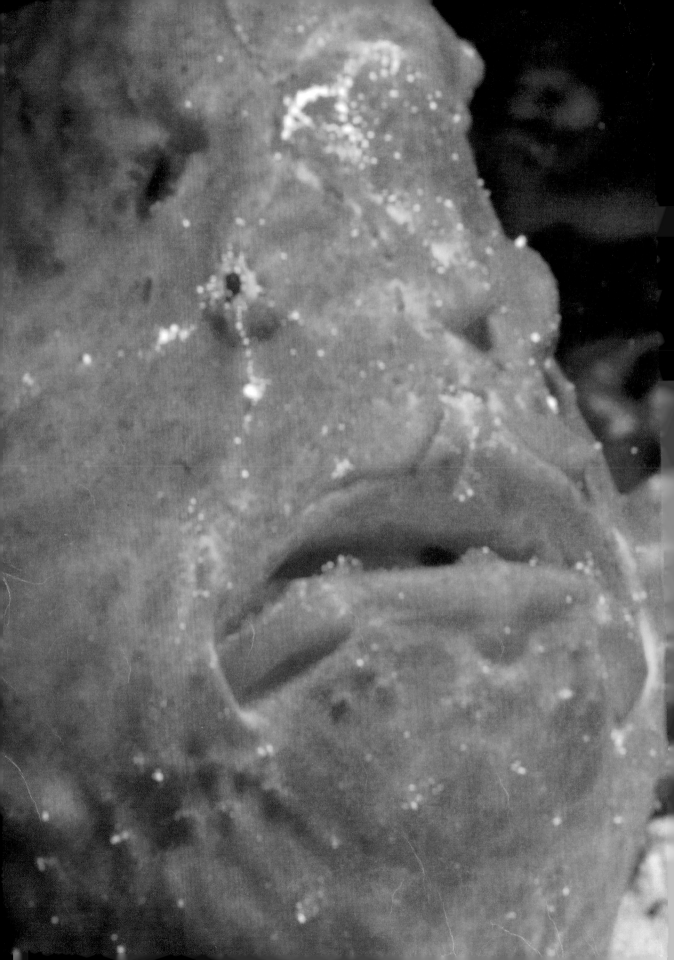

GLOSSARY

barbel (BAHR bel) — long, soft, slender "whiskers" of flesh on the mouths of certain fish

prey (PRAY) — an animal that is hunted by another animal for food

species (SPEE sheez) — within a group of closely related animals, one certain kind, such as a *great white* shark

venom (VEN um) — a poison produced by certain animals, including some fish

Frogfish looks more like a sponge than a fish.

INDEX

FURTHER READING

Find out more about frightening fish with these helpful books:
Ling, Mary. *Amazing Fish.* Knopf, 1991.
Palmer, Sarah. *Great White Sharks.* Rourke, 1988.
Simon, Seymour. *Sharks.* Harper Collins, 1995.
Stone, Lynn. *Giant Sharks.* Rourke, 1996.